ollins

Key Stage 3
Buddhism

Neil McKain
Series Editor: Robert Orme

William Collins' dream of knowledge for all began with the publication of his first book in 1819. A self-educated mill worker, he not only enriched millions of lives, but also founded a flourishing publishing house. Today, staying true to this spirit, Collins books are packed with inspiration, innovation and practical expertise. They place you at the centre of a world of possibility and give you exactly what you need to explore it.

Collins. Freedom to teach

Published by Collins
An imprint of HarperCollins*Publishers*
The News Building
1 London Bridge Street
London SE1 9GF

HarperCollins *Publishers*
1st Floor
Watermarque Building
Ringsend Road
Dublin 4
Ireland

10 9

ISBN 978-0-00-822773-9

Publisher: Joanna Ramsay
Editor: Hannah Dove
Author: Neil McKain
Series Editor: Robert Orme
Development Editor: Sonya Newland
Project manager: Emily Hooton
Copy-editor: Jill Morris
Image researcher: Shelley Noronha
Proof-reader: Ros and Chris Davies
Cover designer: We Are Laura
Cover image: Chonlatip Hirunsatitporn/Shutterstock
Production controller: Rachel Weaver
Typesetter: QBS
Printed and bound in the UK using 100% Renewable Electricity at CPI Group (UK) Ltd

Contents

Introduction

It is not easy to define what makes something a religion. In some religions one god is worshipped, in others many gods are worshipped, and in some no god is worshipped at all. Some religions have a single founder. In others, there is not one person who starts it or one clear moment when it began. To make things more complicated, there are often strong differences of opinion between and even within particular religions. Two people following the same religion can believe opposing things and follow their religion in strikingly different ways. Within any religion, some people build their whole lives around their beliefs while others are less committed to their religion but still think of themselves as part of it. Followers of all religions believe that they have found truth, but their ideas about what is true differ greatly.

Approximately 84 per cent of people in the world today follow a religion and experts predict that this will rise to 87 per cent by 2050. The most followed religion in the UK is Christianity, but there are also followers of many other religions including Islam, Judaism, Buddhism, Hinduism and Sikhism. In recent times there has also been a big increase in the number of people in the UK who do not follow any religion. Some are atheists which means that they do not believe there is a god or gods. Others are agnostics meaning they are not sure if a god or gods exists. Others might believe there is a god or gods, but choose not to belong to a religion.

By studying the beliefs and ways of life of millions of people around the world, you will gain a greater understanding of the past, the modern world and humanity itself. You will explore questions that have troubled humankind through the ages and examine the diverse ways in which these questions have been answered. In a world where religion has and continues to play such a large role, the importance of understanding it is as great as ever.

Robert Orme (Series Editor)

Concise topic introductions set the scene and focus your learning.

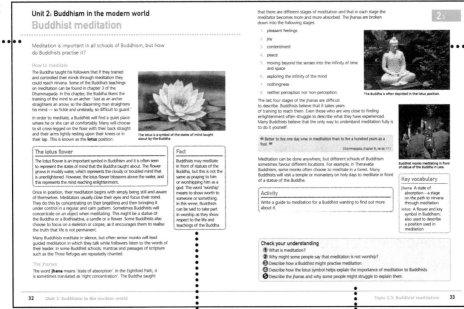

Engaging photos illustrate the key ideas.

Fact boxes provide bite-sized details.

End-of-topic questions are designed to check and consolidate your understanding.

Key fact boxes help you to revise and remember the main points from each unit.

Key vocabulary lists for each unit help you define and remember important terms.

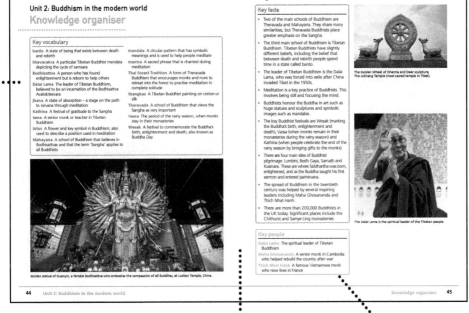

Knowledge organisers can be used to revise and quiz yourself on key dates, definitions and descriptions.

Key people boxes summarise the key figures from the unit.

History and belief

In this book, you will find out about one of the most-followed religions in the world today – Buddhism. In the first half of this book you will discover how Buddhism started and spread. You will see how Buddhism grew from the experiences of an Indian prince called Siddhartha Gautama, who lived 2500 years ago, to a global religion followed by over 500 million people. You will also examine some of the central ideas in the religion which shape the lives of millions of people around the world who call themselves Buddhist.

Unit 1: History and belief
What is Buddhism?

Buddhism began in India more than 2500 years ago.
Who was its founder and what do Buddhists believe?

Buddhism is now the fourth-largest religion in the world. It has approximately 500 million followers, known as Buddhists. There are Buddhists all over the world, but the vast majority (99 per cent) live in Asia. Approximately 200,000 Buddhists live in the UK.

How did Buddhism begin?

Buddhism began in a place called Lumbini in an area of ancient India that is now Nepal. The founder of Buddhism was a prince called Siddhartha Gautama, who was born around 563 BCE. In an effort to understand the truth about life, Siddhartha practised **meditation**. Through this, he eventually achieved **enlightenment**. Afterwards, he travelled around India, sharing what he had learned. People who followed Siddhartha called him the **Buddha** ('awakened one') because they believed that he was awakened to the true nature of reality.

Is the Buddha a god?

The Buddha never claimed to be a god, so, although his teachings are important to Buddhists, they do not believe that he is divine or that he was sent by a god. Buddhist **scriptures** do not mention a creator god. One of the most important sacred texts in Buddhism is the **Dhammapada,** which Buddhists believe is an accurate collection of the Buddha's teachings.

Siddhartha Gautama died at the age of 80. He remains one of the most influential religious figures in history.

Europe
1,330,000

North America
3,860,000

Asia/Pacific
481,290,000

Middle East/North Africa
500,000

Latin America/
Caribbean
410,000

Sub-Saharan Africa
150,000

A map showing the distribution of Buddhists across the world.

What do Buddhists believe?

Unlike many other religions, Buddhists do not necessarily believe in a single creator god or gods. Instead, they focus on personal development. Buddhist temples always contain a statue of the Buddha, and Buddhists sometimes bow to this as a sign of respect, admiration and appreciation for his teachings, but they do not worship him as a god. Some Buddhists say that they pray. However, this does not mean that they pray to a god or ask for divine help. Buddhist prayer may involve personal reflection, often through chanting and making offerings.

Buddhists believe that we are travelling through a continual cycle of birth, death and rebirth. They call this cycle **samsara**. Buddhists believe that when someone dies he or she is reborn. The person's next life may be better or worse, depending on the **karma** he or she has stored up. Good actions in life store up good karma; bad actions store up bad karma. Buddhists aim to escape samsara by achieving enlightenment through meditation, wisdom and living a good life. Buddhists believe that people who escape samsara enter into a state of complete bliss called **parinirvana**.

How do we know about the Buddha?

There is much debate about the details of the Buddha's life. He lived 2500 years ago and, as far as we know, he did not write down any of his teachings or beliefs. These were passed on orally and then collected and recorded by his followers in the centuries after his death.

Many different stories about the Buddha were told and biographies were written by people living in different parts of Asia. The earliest complete biography was written in the first century CE, 500 years after the Buddha's death. Some of the details in biographies of the Buddha's life conflict with each other and historians who study them disagree about whether any of the events in his life really happened. For many Buddhists, the question of whether the events happened historically is not the most important thing. It is the message of the Buddha's life story that is most important to them.

> 66 All that we are is the result of what we have thought: it is founded on our thoughts, it is made up of our thoughts. 99
> Dhammapada chapter 1, verse 1

Key vocabulary

Buddha The awakened or enlightened one

Dhammapada A Buddhist scripture that contains the teachings and sayings of the Buddha

enlightenment The state of being awakened to the truth about life

karma The forces that influence peoples' fortune and future rebirth

meditation The practice of focusing the mind

parinirvana A state of complete bliss, entered into by souls that are not reborn

samsara The continual process of life, death and rebirth

scriptures Religious texts

Check your understanding

1. How many Buddhists are there in the world and where do they live?
2. When and where did Buddhism begin?
3. Explain who Siddhartha Gautama was and how both a historian and a Buddhist might view the events of his life.
4. Explain Buddhist beliefs about samsara.
5. Explain why there might be debate over whether Buddhism is a religion.

Unit 1: History and belief
The early life of Siddhartha Gautama

Siddhartha Gautama was born a prince. What happened in his childhood to suggest that he was destined for a very different life?

Siddhartha's mother, Queen Maya, ruled over one of the sixteen kingdoms in ancient India. According to Buddhist legend, she had a vivid dream while she was pregnant with Siddhartha. In the dream, a white elephant gave her a beautiful lotus flower before entering into her side. The king realised that this dream was important, so he called the **Brahmins** to interpret it. The Brahmins told the king that his son would become either a great and powerful ruler who would conquer the world or a holy teacher and an enlightened being.

Siddhartha's upbringing

Soon after Siddhartha's birth, his mother died. He was raised by his aunt, who treated him as if he were her own son. Siddhartha's early life as a prince was one of luxury and indulgence. His father ensured that his son wanted for nothing, and Siddhartha grew up a healthy, intelligent and contented child.

Siddhartha and the swan

The stories of Siddhartha's early life demonstrate his wisdom and compassion. On one occasion, mentioned in an early biography of the Buddha called the Abhiniskramana Sutra, Siddhartha was playing with some friends in the palace garden. One of the boys was his cousin, Prince Devadatta. Preparing to fight in defence of the kingdom was an essential part of a prince's education, so both boys were skilled archers. While they were playing, Devadatta shot down a swan with his bow and arrow, badly wounding the bird. Devadatta wanted to keep the swan, but Siddhartha refused to give it to his cousin. Instead, he took care of it, and when it had recovered he set it free. In his later teachings, the Buddha emphasised the importance of showing compassion and loving kindness to all living things.

Legends say that right after birth, Siddhartha walked seven steps forward and at each step a lotus flower appeared on the ground.

Siddhartha at the ploughing ceremony

In another story from the same book, Siddhartha attended the annual ploughing ceremony. This ceremony marked the time when new crops would be sown. Following tradition, Siddhartha's father opened the ceremony by driving the first pair of prize cows across the field. The young prince Siddhartha sat down in the shade of a tree and watched everyone. The crowds were cheering and happy, but Siddhartha noticed that while people were having fun the animals were straining under

The ploughing festival, known as Raek Na, still takes place in Thailand each May and marks the start of rice-growing season.

the weight of the plough. The ploughing also brought worms to the surface, which were then eaten by birds. It struck Siddhartha that even a festival, which should be a time of happiness, caused suffering.

After noticing this, Siddhartha fell into a deep meditative trance. He breathed in and out slowly and found that he could focus his mind in a way that helped him better understand himself and the world around him. Meditation would become central to his life as the Buddha. It is a key part of Buddhism today.

> 66 When I was a child, I was delicately brought up, most delicately. A white sunshade was held over me day and night to protect me from cold, heat, dust, dirt, and dew. My father gave me three lotus ponds: one where red lotuses bloomed, one where white lotuses bloomed, one where blue lotuses bloomed. 99
>
> The Buddha, recalling his childhood

Fact

Historians cannot be sure that these events from Siddhartha's childhood really took place. However, the fact that early Buddhists wrote these stories shows that they wanted to demonstrate that the teachings and message of Buddhism were part of Siddhartha's life even before he became known as the Buddha.

A life of luxury

Siddhartha's father did not want his son to become a holy man as the Brahmins had suggested. He wanted him to inherit the kingdom and become a great ruler. He made sure that Siddhartha was brought up in luxury and received the best education. The king also arranged for Siddhartha to marry his cousin, Yashodhara. The royal couple were waited on by servants and only the most beautiful and healthy people in the kingdom were allowed to visit them. They ate the finest foods and wore expensive clothes. One of the many legends about the Buddha says that they spent 10 years on honeymoon in a variety of specially built palaces within the walls of the royal grounds, and Siddhartha was kept entertained by musicians and dancing girls.

Siddhartha and his wife, Yashodhara.

Yashodhara became pregnant and gave birth to a son, Rahula. The king was happy – his son's life was exactly as he had hoped. However, Siddhartha wanted to know what lay beyond the walls of the royal grounds. He asked his servant, Channa, to take him outside and show him what life was really like.

Key vocabulary

Brahmins Priests in ancient India who interpreted Queen Maya's dream when she was pregnant with Siddhartha

Check your understanding

1. How did the Buddha describe his childhood when he looked back on it as an adult?
2. What does the story of the swan tell us about Siddhartha's character?
3. What lesson did Siddhartha learn by watching the ploughing festival?
4. Who were Yashodhara and Rahula?
5. Explain why the king did not want Siddhartha to leave the palace grounds and how he tried to prevent it.

Unit 1: History and belief
The Four Sights and the Great Departure

What did Siddhartha see when he left the grounds of his palace that changed his life forever?

At the age of 29, Siddhartha decided that he wanted to leave the royal grounds for the first time to see what lay beyond its walls. When the king found out that his son wanted to leave, he arranged for Siddhartha to visit one of the royal parks near the palace, but he gave instructions that anyone who was poor, elderly or ill should be kept away. The people were delighted to see their prince and they cheered as Siddhartha made his way along the roads in a chariot.

The Four Sights

The first sight: old age

The gods realised that the king was trying to deceive the future Buddha, so they transformed a member of the crowd into a white-haired old man, bent over with age. Siddhartha had never seen an elderly person before. When he asked Channa about it, Channa explained that everyone must age. Siddhartha sighed deeply, shook his head and said: 'So that is how old age destroys the memory, beauty and the strength of all!'

Siddhartha Gautama and the four sights of old-age, disease, death and an ascetic.

The second sight: sickness

On Siddhartha's next journey, the gods showed him a vision of a diseased man, wailing and groaning in pain. According to the **Pali Canon**, when Channa explained illness to the prince, Siddhartha is said to have 'trembled like the reflection of the moon on rippling water' and said: 'This then is the calamity of disease, which afflicts all. The world sees it but does not lose its confident ways.'

The third sight: death

On the third journey, Siddhartha saw a dead man's body being carried along the road in a funeral procession. The prince asked why the man was not moving and why the people following the procession were crying. Again, Channa explained the sight to him. Upon learning about death for the first time, Siddhartha was filled with dismay. He lost courage and hope, declaring: 'This is the end which has been fixed for all and yet the world forgets its fears and takes no heed.'

From this moment, Siddhartha withdrew from palace life and stopped finding happiness in the luxuries provided for him. He began to think about the true meaning of life and realised that he had much to learn. 'It is not that I despise the objects of the world,' he explained. 'But when I consider the impermanence of everything in this world then I can find no delight in it.'

Siddhartha meets the old man.

The fourth sight: a holy man

On his final journey, the prince rode his horse into the forest, hoping to find peace and solitude for his troubled mind. As he approached the woodland, he saw an **ascetic** man walking – almost gliding – towards him from the trees. The man wore simple robes and explained calmly to Siddhartha that he had given up his home, his possessions and his family to search for an answer to all the suffering and unhappiness in the world. The man then disappeared before the prince's eyes.

The Great Departure

Siddhartha decided that he needed to leave his life as a prince and search for an answer to the question of how to deal with the suffering in the world. He returned to the palace, took a final look at his sleeping wife and son, and then he and Channa left under the cover of night. When Siddhartha reached a refuge in the forest, he removed his jewels and his weapons. He also cut his hair and replaced his royal robes with simple clothes. Siddhartha commanded Channa to return his possessions to his father and then come back to him. Channa begged the prince not to leave, but Siddhartha replied: 'Birds settle on a tree for a while, and then go their separate ways again. Clouds meet and then fly apart again. The meeting of all living beings must likewise inevitably end in their parting.'

After witnessing the Four Sights, Siddhartha left his life of luxury behind him.

Most historians believe that the story of the **Four Sights** is probably not literally or historically true, but it still has great spiritual meaning for Buddhists.

❝ It is hard to believe that the Buddha was as naive as the story portrays him, or that his disenchantment with palace life was nearly as sudden. It might be more useful to read the story as a **parable**. ❞

Damien Keown (Professor of Buddhism), *Buddhism: A Very Short Introduction* (OUP, 2000), p. 19

Activity

Divide your page into four. In each section draw an image to represent one of the Four Sights and explain how it affected Siddhartha.

Key vocabulary

ascetic Someone who lives a life of simplicity and self-denial

Four Sights Four things seen by Siddhartha when leaving the royal grounds – old age, sickness, death and a holy man

Pali Canon The main sacred text for many Buddhists which contains the teachings of the Buddha, rules for monks and nuns and the philosophy of Buddhism; also known as the Tipitaka

parable A story used to teach a moral or spiritual lesson

Check your understanding

1. What were the Four Sights?
2. What did the Four Sights make Siddhartha realise?
3. What did Siddhartha decide to do after encountering all Four Sights?
4. Explain the meaning of Siddhartha's words to Channa about the birds and clouds.
5. 'Siddhartha did the right thing by leaving his life in the palace.' Discuss this statement.

Unit 1: History and belief
The path to enlightenment

Siddhartha spent six years practising meditation and living as an ascetic. How did he eventually achieve enlightenment?

Siddhartha left the palace because he wanted to discover answers to the question of how to overcome suffering. He met two masters of meditation who taught him how to meditate intensively. Siddhartha was an excellent student and greatly impressed the masters, but he did not find the answers that he was looking for. He decided to set off on his own, travelling across India.

Asceticism

While travelling, Siddhartha met five ascetics by the banks of a river. When the ascetics saw how gifted Siddhartha was at meditation, they decided to become his followers. Siddhartha spent the next six years of his life living as an ascetic. Ascetics would punish their body in order to try and gain peace and wisdom. This could involve fasting, standing on one foot for a long time and sleeping on nails. Siddhartha hoped that denying his body the things it wanted would help free his mind to find the answers he was searching for.

This statue shows Siddhartha during the time when he was starving himself.

First, Siddhartha learned how to control his breath. He practised holding his breath for as long as possible, but this made him suffer from headaches and exhaustion. Next, he decided to starve himself. Buddhist legends say that he survived on only a spoonful of soup, a single seed or a single grain of rice each day. Soon, Siddhartha became ill. He was unable to stand or even sit upright, his hair fell out and his bones began to be visible through his skin. Siddhartha realised that he would die if he continued without enough food, so he decided to give up his ascetic life. His five ascetic followers found him eating and so abandoned him, thinking he loved luxury too much.

The Middle Way

Siddhartha's asceticism led him to an important truth. He realised that denying his body what it needed was as bad as being surrounded by luxury. Neither extreme brought him any closer to finding the answers he was looking for. He saw that the only way to reach peace was to follow the **Middle Way** – a life of moderation, in which he had neither too much nor too little of anything. This is a key principle that Buddhists try to live by today.

After abandoning the ascetic lifestyle, Siddhartha visited the north Indian city of **Bodh Gaya**. He was still weak from his years of self-denial. One day he went down to the river to bathe and met a young girl. She was shocked by his withered appearance and overcome by his holiness. The girl offered Siddhartha some rice milk, which he accepted willingly. The milk gave Siddhartha some strength. He put aside the rags he had been wearing and sat down, cross-legged, in the shade of a Bodhi tree. He began to meditate, saying: 'I will not move from this spot until I have found supreme and final wisdom.'

The defeat of Mara

While Siddhartha was meditating, the demon Lord Mara began to attack him. Mara sent his three daughters to tempt Siddhartha. He resisted them. Next, Mara tried to convince Siddhartha that it was wrong for him to abandon his family. Still, Siddhartha refused to move. Mara then unleashed a host of demons and monsters on Siddhartha. Still, Siddhartha did not move. Finally, Mara ordered Siddhartha: 'Arise from that seat! It belongs to me.' Siddhartha said nothing, but lowered one of his hands to touch the earth. As he did so, the sky filled with thunder and the earth shook. Mara had been defeated.

Lord Mara attacking Siddhartha.

Siddhartha was finally free to achieve his goal of enlightenment. Through deep meditation, he gained the ability to remove all greed, hatred and delusion. He had found **nirvana** and become the Buddha.

Fact

Some Buddhists interpret the story of Mara literally, as a historical event – they think that there was an actual demon spirit who tried to stop Siddhartha from meditating. Other Buddhists see Mara as a symbolic character, representing the desires and temptations of the mind that people need to remove if they are to achieve enlightenment.

The three stages of enlightenment

Siddhartha's enlightenment is said to have happened in three stages over the course of one night. During the first stage, he saw all of the many animal and human lives that he had lived before. In the second stage, he saw the complete cycle of samsara, which was like a wheel constantly spinning. Siddhartha realised that the cycle of death and rebirth of all beings in the universe is determined by their karma. In the final stage, Siddhartha achieved enlightenment.

Key vocabulary

Bodh Gaya The holiest site in Buddhism, where Siddhartha meditated under a Bodhi tree and became the Buddha

Middle Way A lifestyle between luxury and having nothing at all

nirvana A state of bliss experienced by those who have found enlightenment

Check your understanding

1. Why did Siddhartha become an ascetic?
2. Describe the methods of self-denial that Siddhartha tried.
3. What is the Middle Way?
4. Explain two different ways in which the story of Mara can be interpreted.
5. Explain how Siddhartha achieved enlightenment.

Unit 1: History and belief
The Four Noble Truths

What truths did the Buddha teach others to help them achieve enlightenment?

After Siddhartha reached enlightenment he stayed in Bodh Gaya for weeks, wondering what he should do next. He realised that he needed to share the truths that he had discovered, but did not know how best to do this.

The dharma

The Buddha said that he did not create any new ideas – he simply tried to explain how the world was. The name that Buddhists give to the laws or truths that Buddha discovered is the **dharma**. At first, the Buddha was unsuccessful in sharing the dharma. One story tells how he met a man who asked him 'Who is your teacher?' The Buddha replied that he had no teacher and had reached enlightenment on his own. The man walked away, unimpressed. This story shows that the Buddha remained an ordinary man after his enlightenment. He did not become a god.

The first sermon

After several weeks, the Buddha left Bodh Gaya and travelled 200 miles to a city called Sarnath, near the river Ganges. He came to a deer park in the city where he found the five followers who had abandoned him. They were still living as ascetics and were sceptical of their former leader's claim to have achieved enlightenment. In the deer park, the Buddha preached his first **sermon** to the five men, explaining what he had learned under the Bodhi tree. This sermon is known as 'Setting in Motion the Wheel of the Dharma' and its teachings are known as the **Four Noble Truths**, and are the basis of Buddhism.

The Four Noble Truths

1. All creatures suffer

In the first Noble Truth, Buddha taught that life is not how we would like it to be, and this causes us suffering. The **Sanskrit** word for this is dukkha. As well as suffering, dukkha is sometimes translated as dissatisfaction or stress.

The Buddha realised that even when we do find happiness it only lasts for a fleeting moment before we become dissatisfied again. He taught that many people try to ignore or deny this truth, but in order to overcome suffering they must accept it.

2. Suffering is caused by selfish desires

In the second Noble Truth, the Buddha taught that selfish desires and cravings are the cause of all suffering. This craving might be for material

> **Fact**
>
> Buddhist philosophy is underpinned by three key ideas. These are sometimes referred to as the three universal truths:
>
> - anicca – everything changes
> - anatta – there is no permanent self
> - **dukkha** – everything suffers.

A statue showing Siddhartha preaching to the five ascetics who abandoned him.

> ❝ Birth is suffering, decay, sickness and death are suffering. To be separated from what you like is suffering. To want something and not get it is suffering. ❞
>
> The Buddha

things, for people, or even for immortality. We might be temporarily satisfied, but this is short lived because everything that exists is constantly changing or turning like a wheel. Nothing is permanent, so even when our desires are fulfilled we do not gain lasting peace and satisfaction. To achieve enlightenment, therefore, we must stop allowing ourselves to be controlled by selfish desires or cravings because these desires are at odds with reality, which is always changing.

3. Suffering can be ended

The third Noble Truth is the idea that because we are the cause of our own suffering we can also overcome it and achieve enlightenment like the Buddha. Reaching nirvana requires us to eliminate all greed, hatred and delusion, which are called the **Three Poisons**.

4. The way to end suffering is to follow the Eightfold Path

In the fourth Noble Truth, the Buddha provided eight instructions for people to follow in order to be free from suffering and reach enlightenment. These instructions are known as the **Eightfold Path**. This path provides a guide to how Buddhists should live their lives.

The Buddha is seen as a guide. His teachings help people understand why we suffer.

The analogy of the doctor

One way of understanding the Four Noble Truths is through the following analogy. If you are ill then you go the doctor. The doctor will (1) see what the problem is, (2) understand its cause, (3) decide on a cure and (4) prescribe a way of making you better. This is why Buddhists sometimes think the Buddha is like a doctor whose mission is to help remove suffering from the world.

Key vocabulary

dharma The Buddha's teachings

dukkha The suffering or dissatisfaction of all living beings

Eightfold Path Eight instructions taught by the Buddha to help people overcome suffering and reach enlightenment

Four Noble Truths The basis of the Buddha's teachings: all creatures suffer; suffering is caused by selfish desires; suffering can be ended; the way to end suffering is to follow the Eightfold Path

Sanskrit An ancient Indian language

sermon A speech given by a religious leader

Three Poisons Greed, hatred and delusion

The Buddha is seen as a guide.

Check your understanding

1. What is meant by 'dharma'?
2. Why is the symbol of the wheel important to Buddhists?
3. What are the Four Noble Truths?
4. Explain each of the Four Noble Truths in your own words.
5. Explain how the analogy of the doctor helps explain the Four Noble Truths.

Unit 1: History and belief
The Eightfold Path

How does the Eightfold Path guide Buddhists on how to live in order to reach nirvana?

The Eightfold Path is not a set of rules that people must follow in order to please an almighty god. Buddhists do not believe that their actions are judged by a god. The path consists of eight steps to help people achieve a contented life. By following the Eightfold Path, Buddhists believe they can overcome the selfish desires that cause all suffering. It directs people to think, speak and act in better ways, which helps them to achieve inner peace and eliminate suffering.

The eight parts all fit together and should not be taken individually. No step is more important than any other. Buddhists believe that the steps should be developed and practised in their day-to-day lives.

The Spring Temple Buddha statue in China is one of the tallest statues in the world. The Buddha's right hand is held up with his palm facing outwards. This symbolises a shield, representing the fact that the Buddha offers protection from suffering.

The Eightfold Path

1. Right understanding

This first step in the Eightfold Path can also be translated as 'right view' and means to see things clearly and to understand them. The Buddha taught his followers that they must understand and accept the Four Noble Truths and that all living creatures are in a cycle of birth, death and rebirth (samsara).

2. Right thought

The Buddha taught that people should devote their lives to thinking in the right way in order to remove selfish desires and hatred. People should focus their mind on compassionate thoughts and developing wisdom rather than selfish thoughts that cause suffering.

3. Right speech

The Buddha taught that people should always speak truthfully and compassionately. Unkind words, swearing, lies and gossip should be avoided. This step also involves knowing when to speak and when to remain silent.

4. Right action

The fourth step is sometimes translated as 'right conduct', which means acting in the right way. The Buddha taught that people should act in a compassionate way that avoids causing harm. In particular, the Buddha said that people should avoid killing, stealing and any other action that causes harm to themselves or another living being (including animals).

5. Right livelihood

Livelihood refers to the work or job that you do to make money. The Buddha taught that people should avoid jobs that involve causing harm or encourage dishonesty.

6. Right effort

The final three steps on the path are about training your mind. Right effort means making an effort to be aware and in control of what is happening in your mind. People should limit and dispose of harmful thoughts. Instead, they should focus on positive thoughts.

7. Right mindfulness

This is sometimes translated as right awareness. People should train their mind to be fully aware of their thoughts and actions as well as being conscious of others around them. Some Buddhists talk about being aware or 'mindful' of the present moment. Buddhists try to avoid distracting thoughts about the past or the future.

The symbol of the wheel has eight spokes representing the Eightfold Path.

8. Right concentration

To train their minds fully, people must practise meditation. Buddhists use a variety of meditation techniques in order to calm the mind, understand reality and guide them in their day-to-day lives.

The analogy of the path

The Buddha taught that by following the Eightfold Path correctly people could escape the suffering experienced in samsara. The path offers a way to shape life in pursuit of wisdom, truth and virtue, and leads to a place to which, deep down, everyone wants to go. It is a path to enlightenment. The path is not a straight one, nor is it easy to navigate. Buddhists believe that people must follow the path in their own way and that they will almost certainly stumble or fall as they journey through life.

The path leading to the Buddha at Fo Guang Shan Buddha Museum, Taiwan.

Activity

Create a flow chart to summarise the Eightfold Path. Add bullet points to explain what each step requires and give examples from everyday life if you can.

Check your understanding

1. What is the Eightfold Path?
2. How does a wheel symbolise the Eightfold Path?
3. Explain each step of the path in your own words.
4. Explain how following the Eightfold Path is different from following a set of rules in another religion that you know about.
5. 'The Buddha should be remembered as a great religious leader.' Discuss this statement.

Unit 1: History and belief
What is the Sangha?

As he travelled around India, the Buddha attracted many followers. How did these followers honour the Buddha and follow his teachings?

The first Buddhists

The first Buddhist community was established in Sarnath, but the Buddha and his early disciples travelled around northern India, spreading the dharma. Many people were attracted to the Buddha's message because it offered freedom from suffering. It especially appealed to lower-class people, who experienced great hardship. At the time of the Buddha, Indian society was governed by the **caste system**. Everybody belonged to a caste, which determined what sort of job they did and the kind of life they led. People were born into a caste and could not leave it. The most respected caste was priests (Brahmins). Below them were the warriors. This was the caste that the Buddha had been born into. Beneath them were farmers and then servants. At the bottom were the Untouchables: social outcasts that nobody would associate with.

The Buddha's teachings went against the caste system. He taught that caste and social hierarchy were irrelevant – all beings are part of the same cycle of samsara.

The Three Jewels

As more people began to follow the Buddha's message, a community of monks and nuns was established. This became known as the **Sangha**. The first monks, called **bhikkhus**, were the five ascetics who had previously abandoned Siddhartha, but became his followers again after his sermon in the deer park.

In the early days of Buddhism monks and nuns followed the same rules. Those who joined the Sangha were required to shave their heads, wear simple orange or yellow robes and recite the **Three Jewels** (so called because they are very precious and give light to people):

> " What makes you noble is if you understand reality, you know if you're a good person. If you're a wise person then you're noble. "
> The Buddha

Bhikkhus receiving alms.

> " …and good it is to serve the monks… "
> The Buddha (in the Dhammapada)

I take refuge in the Buddha.   I take refuge in the dharma.   I take refuge in the Sangha.

The Three Jewels are also known as the Three Refuges. A refuge is a place where people are safe from harm. Buddhists find refuge in the example of the Buddha, who found nirvana on his own and discovered the meaning of life. They also find refuge in the dharma, the teachings of the Buddha. The Sangha is the community of monks and nuns who founded monasteries – places of safety where people could go to study and practise Buddhism.

Bhikkhus relaxing outside a temple in Cambodia.

The Five Precepts

All Buddhists are expected to follow the **Five Precepts**, which means observing these rules:

- not to take the life of any living being
- not to take what is not given
- not to take part in sexual misconduct
- not to speak falsely
- not to take drugs that cloud the mind.

From the start, monks also had to follow strict rules that developed from the Eightfold Path. The Sangha was seen as the living representation of the Buddha's teachings and so its members led a strict and disciplined life. As the Sangha grew, so did the number of rules. The only possessions a monk could have were robes to wear, a bowl to collect food in and a razor to shave with.

Bhikkhus meditating in Thailand.

The Sangha today

When Buddhists join the Sangha today, they follow more rules than the **laity**. Once they are full members, there are over two hundred rules to follow, but during their training they have just five rules in addition to the Five Precepts. These are:

- not to eat after midday
- not to sing, dance or play music
- not to wear perfume or jewellery
- not to sit on high chairs or sleep on a soft bed
- not to accept or use money.

The Sangha is highly respected by Buddhists today and some Buddhists believe that only monks can achieve nirvana.

Key vocabulary

bhikkhu A Buddhist monk; nuns are called bhikkhunis

caste system A series of social classes that determine someone's job and status in society

Five Precepts Five rules that all Buddhists are expected to follow

laity Buddhists who are not monks or nuns

Sangha The community of Buddhist monks and nuns

Three Jewels Buddha, dharma, Sangha; also known as the Three Refuges

Check your understanding

1. What is the Sangha?
2. What are the Three Jewels?
3. Why did the Buddha disagree with the caste system?
4. What are the Five Precepts?
5. Explain why members of the Sangha have to live by stricter rules than other Buddhists. Use examples in your answer.

The spread of Buddhism

How did an Indian emperor help Buddhism spread to new lands 200 years after the Buddha's death?

The death of the Buddha

After recruiting followers and establishing the Sangha, the Buddha continued to travel around northern India sharing his teachings. He did this even in old age when his health was failing.

The Buddha's followers were distraught as their leader approached death. However, the Buddha used his final moments to share an important teaching with them: 'He who sees me sees the teaching and he who sees the teaching sees me.' The Buddha did not appoint anyone to succeed him as Buddhist leader. Instead, he told the monks that the dharma would be their guide, and that he would always be there in the dharma.

Following this, the Buddha fell into a meditative trance and finally achieved parinirvana – complete nirvana. Stories tell of how the 'earth quivered like a ship struck by a storm' and beautiful flowers blossomed on the trees above where the Buddha had laid down, showering his body with their petals. The Buddha's body was cremated and the remains divided up and put into eight **stupas**. The stupas became holy sites of **pilgrimage** as Buddhism spread.

> 66 In measured steps the Best of Men walked to this final resting place – no more return in store for him, no further suffering. In full sight of his disciples he lay down on his right side, rested his head on his hand, and put one leg over the other. 99
>
> A description of the death of the Buddha, from the Pali Canon

The Reclining Buddha in South Korea. It is believed that you can gain good fortune by touching the Buddha's feet.

> ### Fact
>
> Buddhism began in northern India, where people were Hindu. It never became the official religion there, but it was popular for more than 1000 years after the Buddha's death. As Islam expanded into India from the eighth century CE, Buddhism's popularity began to decline, but by this time it had already spread to other parts of the world.

Emperor Ashoka

In the third century BCE, an Indian emperor named Ashoka became the world's first Buddhist ruler. His conversion had a profound impact on the development of Buddhism.

Ashoka ruled over large parts of India. Like his father and grandfather, Ashoka wanted to expand his empire, and he waged many wars to achieve this. In one battle, Ashoka's army captured around 150,000 people and made them slaves; they killed 100,000 more. When Ashoka heard about this bloodthirsty incident he was horrified by the role he had played. He decided that he would no longer follow in the violent footsteps of his father and grandfather. Instead, he would rule his empire according to the Buddhist principles of non-violence and compassion, which he had learned from a Buddhist monk.

Ashoka abandoned his attempts to expand his empire and focused on finding ways to care for the people he already ruled. This involved building hospitals, schools and even digging wells to provide water for thirsty travellers passing through. He also banned the killing of animals. All over his empire, he ordered that pillars and rocks be engraved with words of encouragement for people to behave in a humble, honest and generous way. Although he favoured Buddhism himself, Ashoka insisted that all religions should be tolerated in his empire.

Ashoka built statues around his empire promoting Buddhist virtues.

Buddhism spreads

Ashoka sent **missionaries** to spread the Buddhist message. These missionaries travelled as far as Egypt, Syria and Macedonia. However, they were most successful in Sri Lanka. According to Buddhist tradition, Ashoka even sent his son and daughter as missionaries to Sri Lanka, where they were warmly welcomed by the ruler, King Tissa. Ashoka's daughter took with her a cutting from the Bodhi tree where the Buddha had achieved enlightenment. Although the original tree that grew from this cutting no longer stands, a tree that is believed to be a descendant of it is a popular place of Buddhist pilgrimage today.

In the centuries after the Buddha's death, his teachings were passed on orally. Some were carved into stone by Ashoka, but many were not. Buddhist teachings were first written down by Sri Lankan monks in 29 BCE. They were called the Pali Canon.

> ### Key vocabulary
>
> **missionaries** People who spread a religious message to different countries
>
> **pilgrimage** A journey taken to a place of religious importance
>
> **stupa** A place where the remains of the Buddha were buried

Check your understanding

1 Describe the death of the Buddha.
2 Who was Emperor Ashoka?
3 Explain why Ashoka became a Buddhist.
4 Why is Ashoka such a respected ruler? Give examples.
5 How did Buddhism spread beyond India? Include the word 'missionary' in your answer.

Unit 1: History and belief
Knowledge organiser

Key vocabulary

ascetic Someone who lives a life of simplicity and self-denial

bhikkhu A Buddhist monk; nuns are called bhikkhunis

Bodh Gaya The holiest site in Buddhism, where Siddhartha meditated under a Bodhi tree and became the Buddha

Brahmins Priests in ancient India who interpreted Queen Maya's dream when she was pregnant with Siddhartha

Buddha The awakened or enlightened one

caste system A series of social classes that determine someone's job and status in society

Dhammapada A Buddhist scripture that contains the teachings and sayings of the Buddha

dharma The Buddha's teachings

dukkha The suffering or dissatisfaction of all living beings

Eightfold Path Eight instructions taught by the Buddha to help people overcome suffering and reach enlightenment

enlightenment The state of being awakened to the truth about life

Five Precepts Five rules that all Buddhists are expected to follow

Four Noble Truths The basis of the Buddha's teachings: all creatures suffer; suffering is caused by selfish desires; suffering can be ended; the way to end suffering is to follow the Eightfold Path

Four Sights Four things seen by Siddhartha when leaving the royal grounds – old age, sickness, death and a holy man

karma The forces that influence people's fortune and future rebirth

laity Buddhists who are not monks or nuns

meditation The practice of focusing the mind

Middle Way A lifestyle between luxury and having nothing at all

missionaries People who spread a religious message to different countries

nirvana A state of bliss experienced by those who have found enlightenment

Pali Canon The main sacred text for many Buddhists which contains the teachings of the Buddha, rules for monks and nuns and the philosophy of Buddhism; also known as the Tipitaka

parable A story used to teach a moral or spiritual lesson

parinirvana A state of complete bliss, entered into by souls that are not reborn

pilgrimage A journey taken to a place of religious importance

samsara The continual process of life, death and rebirth

Sangha The community of Buddhist monks and nuns

Sanskrit An ancient Indian language

scriptures Religious texts

sermon A speech given by a religious leader

stupa A place where the remains of the Buddha were buried

Three Jewels Buddha, dharma, Sangha; also known as the Three Refuges

Three Poisons Greed, hatred and delusion

Key facts

- Buddhism began in India over 2500 years ago. It is now the fourth-largest religion in the world, with approximately 500 million followers. 99% of Buddhists live in Asia. 50% live in China.

- Buddhists believe that everyone is travelling through a cycle of birth, death and rebirth called samsara. A person's actions in this life can affect his or her next one (karma).

- The main sacred text for Buddhists is the Pali Canon, which contains Buddhist philosophy and teachings.

- Buddhism was founded by a prince called Siddhartha Gautama. From childhood, Siddhartha noticed the suffering of other creatures.

- When he was 29 years old, Siddhartha saw four things that changed his view of life: old age, sickness, death and a holy man. He gave up his life of luxury and set out to discover how to end suffering by living as an ascetic.

- Siddhartha eventually realised that denying his body what it needed was as bad as living in luxury. He settled on the Middle Way. Eventually, while sitting under a Bodhi tree, he found enlightenment, nirvana, and became the Buddha.

- The Buddha attracted many followers. They eventually established the Sangha, a community of monks and nuns who dedicate their lives to Buddhism.

- The basis of the Buddha's teachings are the Four Noble Truths: all creatures suffer; suffering is caused by selfish desires; suffering can be ended; the way to end suffering is to follow the Eightfold Path.

- The Eightfold Path is a series of eight steps that Buddhists can follow to help them lead a contented life.

- All Buddhists follow the Five Precepts. Members of the Sangha follow over two hundred more rules, but when they first join there are just five extra rules.

- After the Buddha's death, Buddhism spread to other countries with the help of the Indian Emperor Ashoka, who converted to Buddhism and encouraged it across his large empire.

Key people

Ashoka An Indian emperor who ruled between 272 and 231 BCE and became the first Buddhist ruler

the Buddha The name given to Siddhartha Gautama, an Indian prince born in 563 BCE, after he achieved enlightenment; the central figure of Buddhism

Channa Siddhartha's servant

Devadatta Siddhartha's cousin

Mara The demon Lord who tried to prevent Siddhartha from achieving enlightenment under the Bodhi tree

Maya Siddhartha's mother

Rahula Siddhartha's son

Siddhartha Gautama An Indian prince born in 563 BCE who became the Buddha. He died in 486 BCE

Yashodhara Siddhartha Gautama's cousin and wife

Tian Tan Buddha, also known as the Big Buddha, is a large bronze statue located in Hong Kong. It was completed in 1993.

Buddhism in the modern world

Buddhists do not all believe the same things and they follow the religion in many different ways. In the second half of this book, you will examine the different schools of Buddhism in the world today. You will explore how Buddhist beliefs are expressed through meditation, art, festivals and pilgrimage. You will also see how Buddhists have suffered persecution and some Buddhist leaders have been forced to flee their countries. Today, there are Buddhists living in many different countries, far from where Buddhism began. In the final topic of the book, you will discover what life is like for Buddhists living in the UK.

What are the schools of Buddhism?

Buddhism is a diverse religion, with many different branches.
What are the major schools of Buddhism and how do they differ?

In the centuries after the Buddha's death, Buddhism spread rapidly beyond India. As the dharma (Buddha's teaching) reached different countries, a variety of schools, or branches, of Buddhism developed. The two main schools are **Theravada** Buddhism and **Mahayana** Buddhism. Both follow the basic teaching of the Four Noble Truths and the Eightfold Path. They also both promote showing compassion and loving kindness to all living beings. However, there are differences – as there are between followers of many religions – because people have interpreted the Buddha's teachings differently over time. Despite their differences, scholars often highlight how much the various schools of Buddhism also have in common.

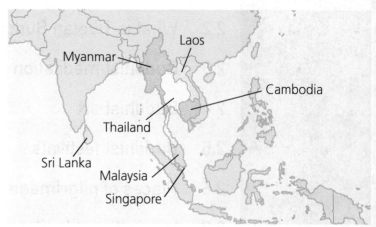

This map shows the countries where Theravada Buddhism is mainly practise

Theravada Buddhism

Theravada Buddhism can mainly be found in Sri Lanka, Thailand, Myanmar (Burma), Laos and Cambodia. It places special emphasis on the role of the Sangha.

Monks have an important part to play in learning and practising the dharma (see page 16) and mastering meditation. Members of the Sangha are able to concentrate fully on following the dharma because they have left their homes and families behind to live in a monastery. Most Theravada Buddhists accept that it would be impossible for everyone live in this way, but they believe that monks and nuns are more likely than the laity to find nirvana.

> **❝** For a vast majority of Buddhists in Theravadin countries, the order of monks is seen by lay Buddhists as a means of gaining the most merit in the hope of accumulating good karma for a better rebirth. **❞**
> Merv Fowler, *Buddhist Beliefs and Practices* (Sussex Academic Press, 1999), p. 65

Householders

The laity in Theravada Buddhism are often called 'householders'. They support the Sangha in a variety of ways, including making offerings (alms) to the community of monks of food, clothes and even money. Householders are also required to provide the monks with the 'eight requisites'. These are the only personal items that a member of the Sangha is allowed:

- an outer robe
- an inner robe
- a thicker robe for winter
- an alms bowl for gathering food

- a razor
- a needle and thread
- a belt
- a water strainer.

Novice monks with their bowls. These are used to collect food from the laity.

Today, it is not uncommon for monks and nuns to have extra items. These range from simple things like towels, socks or sandals to devices like mobile phones. Whatever they have, it must be shared freely with others, and used for good.

Householders are generous towards the monks because they believe that their presence in the community as teachers and preservers of Buddha's teaching is very important. In return for this support, monks serve the laity by conducting religious rituals such as funerals and by providing instruction in meditation, or schooling. For example, in Thailand, many boys leave home and travel to a nearby monastery to live as a novice monk for a year. As well as learning more about Buddhism, they are taught basic numeracy and literacy, and sometimes even computer skills.

The Tipitaka

Theravada Buddhism is based on a collection of writings called the Pali Canon or the Tipitaka. The Pali Canon is divided into three parts, or 'baskets'. The first basket contains the rules of the Sangha. This community of monks and nuns is very important to Theravadins. The second basket contains the teachings and sayings of the Buddha, including the Dhammapada. The third basket interprets and explains the dharma – the Buddha's teachings.

In Mahayana Buddhism the Bodhisattva Avalokitesvara – a Bodhisattva who is believed to have possessed the compassion shown by all Buddhas (those who have achieved nirvana) – is sometimes depicted with 11 faces.

Mahayana Buddhism

There are many different forms of Mahayana Buddhism, which is most popular in China, Taiwan, Japan, Korea and Tibet. Mahayana Buddhists feel that the term 'Sangha' applies to all Buddhists and that everyone has an equal chance of achieving enlightenment.

While paying special attention to monks and nuns, Mahayana Buddhists also focus on **Bodhisattvas**. A Bodhisattva is someone who has reached enlightenment, but, filled with compassion for the suffering of others, chooses not to enter parinirvana. Instead, he or she is reborn into the world to guide and teach others so that they too can reach enlightenment. There are potentially many thousands of Bodhisattvas. Some are greatly respected by Mahayana Buddhists and are often represented in Buddhist art.

Key vocabulary

Bodhisattva A person who has found enlightenment but is reborn to help others

Mahayana A school of Buddhism that believes in Bodhisattvas and that the term 'Sangha' applies to all Buddhists

Theravada A school of Buddhism that views the Sangha as very important

Check your understanding

1 What are the two major schools of Buddhism and where are they found?

2 Describe what life is like for a monk.

3 Explain why Theravada Buddhism places great emphasis on the Sangha.

4 What role do 'householders' play in Theravada Buddhism? Give examples.

5 How does Mahayana Buddhism differ from Theravada? Give at least two reasons and refer to Bodhisattvas in your answer.

What is Tibetan Buddhism?

Who is the leader of Tibetan Buddhism and how is it practised?

Tibetan Buddhism and Shamanism

Tibet is located in a mountainous area in the Himalayas that borders two vast countries: India to the south and China to the north. Buddhism was brought to Tibet by Indian missionaries in the mid-seventh century CE. Tibetan Buddhism exists within the Mahayana tradition and developed alongside another type of spiritual belief called Shamanism. A shaman is someone who believes he or she can control evil spirits and heal the sick. Traditionally, Buddhism rejects such practices, but their importance to Tibetan culture influenced the way that Buddhism developed there.

This map shows where Mahayana Buddhism is practised. Tibetan Buddhism is found within the Mahayana school.

The Tibetan Book of the Dead

Buddhists believe that all beings are part of the cycle of samsara. Different schools of Buddhism have different ideas about what happens after we die and how we are reborn. Some think that rebirth happens immediately. The Tibetan school teaches that in between death and rebirth people spend time in a state called **bardo**. This is described in the Tibetan Book of the Dead (Bardo Thodol), which explains how after someone dies his or her mind can still experience sights, sounds, smells and tastes. It is this attachment to the senses that causes people to be reborn rather than reach parinirvana.

The book also describes how, after death, people come to stand before Yama, King of the Dead. Yama holds up a mirror, showing them all the actions of their life. Some other religions teach that after death we must face judgement for our actions on earth. However, Tibetan Buddhists do not believe they are judged by Yama – he provides the means for people to judge themselves.

> 66 The mirror in which Yama seems to read your past is your own memory, and also his judgement is your own. It is you who pronounce your own judgement, which in turn determines your next rebirth. 99
>
> Tibetan Book of the Dead

Fact

In Tibet, you can often see colourful flags hung from temples and monasteries with prayers and **mantras** written on them. Buddhists believe that the wind carries these words around the world over and over again.

The Tibetan Sangha

In Tibetan Buddhism senior monks are called **lamas**, which means 'teachers'. Monks play an important role in Tibetan society. It is estimated that in the nineteenth century one in six of all men in Tibet were monks and many families expected at least one of their sons to become a monk. Training was intense and took more than 15 years to complete. In most Buddhist countries, monks tended to live away from the world. However, in Tibet, they often worked in trade and politics, and people sometimes asked monks to settle legal disputes. In addition to this, monks spent their time memorising and interpreting sacred texts, practising meditation and maintaining the temples.

The Chinese occupation of Tibet

From the seventeenth century, the **Dalai Lamas** were the spiritual and political leaders of Tibet. This changed in the 1950s, when the Chinese army invaded and occupied Tibet, claiming it was part of China. Fearing capture, the Dalai Lama fled to Dharamsala in India. Many hundreds of monks and other devoted Buddhists followed him on this treacherous journey over the Himalayan mountains into exile. The Dalai Lama still lives in Dharamsala as the head of a Tibetan government and people in exile. Since he left, many Tibetan monasteries have been destroyed or closed down.

Prayer flags near Potala Palace in Tibet, which is where the Dalai Lamas lived until 1959.

Tibetan Buddhists believe that the Dalai Lama is the Bodhisattva Avalokitesvara reborn.

The Dalai Lama

The title Dalai Lama roughly translates as 'ocean of wisdom'. The current Dalai Lama was born as Lhamo Thondup in 1935. Tibetan Buddhists believe he is the fourteenth reincarnation of a Bodhisattva who originally became enlightened in the fourteenth century. The Dalai Lama regularly travels around the world to meet Buddhist and world leaders. He writes books and gives sermons on spiritual issues and communicates with his followers through social media and the internet.

Key vocabulary

bardo A state of being that exists between death and rebirth

Dalai Lama The leader of Tibetan Buddhism, believed to be an incarnation of the Bodhisattva Avalokitesvara

lama A senior monk or teacher in Tibetan Buddhism

mantra A sacred phrase that is chanted during meditation

Check your understanding

1. When did Buddhism reach Tibet?
2. What is Shamanism?
3. Explain Tibetan Buddhist teachings about rebirth. Include a quotation from the Tibetan Book of the Dead in your answer.
4. Why does the current Dalai Lama live in India and not Tibet?
5. Why is the Dalai Lama an important religious leader? Give examples to support your points.

Buddhist meditation

Meditation is important in all schools of Buddhism, but how do Buddhists practise it?

How to meditate

The Buddha taught his followers that if they trained and controlled their minds through meditation they could reach nirvana. Some of the Buddha's teachings on meditation can be found in chapter 3 of the Dhammapada. In this chapter, the Buddha likens the training of the mind to an archer: 'Just as an archer straightens an arrow, so the discerning man straightens his mind — so fickle and unsteady, so difficult to guard.'

In order to meditate, a Buddhist will find a quiet place where he or she can sit comfortably. Many will choose to sit cross-legged on the floor with their back straight and their arms lightly resting upon their knees or in their lap. This is known as the **lotus** position.

The lotus is a symbol of the states of mind taught about by the Buddha.

The lotus flower

The lotus flower is an important symbol in Buddhism and it is often seen to represent the states of mind that the Buddha taught about. The flower grows in muddy water, which represents the cloudy or troubled mind that is unenlightened. However, the lotus flower blossoms above the water, and this represents the mind reaching enlightenment.

Once in position, their meditation begins with simply being still and aware of themselves. Meditators usually close their eyes and focus their mind. They do this by concentrating on their breathing and then bringing it under control in a regular and calm pattern. Sometimes Buddhists will concentrate on an object when meditating. This might be a statue of the Buddha or a Bodhisattva, a candle or a flower. Some Buddhists also choose to focus on a skeleton or corpse, as it encourages them to realise the truth that life is not permanent.

Many Buddhists meditate in silence, but often senior monks will lead guided meditation in which they talk while followers listen to the words of their leader. In some Buddhist schools, mantras and passages of scripture such as the Three Refuges are repeatedly chanted.

The jhanas

The word **jhana** means 'state of absorption'. In the Eightfold Path, it is sometimes translated as 'right concentration'. The Buddha taught

Fact

Buddhists may meditate in front of statues of the Buddha, but this is not the same as praying to him or worshipping him as a god. The word 'worship' means to show worth to someone or something. In this sense, Buddhists can be said to take part in worship as they show respect to the life and teachings of the Buddha.

that there are different stages of meditation and that in each stage the meditator becomes more and more absorbed. The jhanas are broken down into the following stages:

1. pleasant feelings
2. joy
3. contentment
4. peace
5. moving beyond the senses into the infinity of time and space
6. exploring the infinity of the mind
7. nothingness
8. neither perception nor non-perception.

The Buddha is often depicted in the lotus position.

The last four stages of the jhanas are difficult to describe. Buddhists believe that it takes years of training to reach them. Even those who are very close to finding enlightenment often struggle to describe what they have experienced. Many Buddhists believe that the only way to understand meditation fully is to do it yourself.

> 66 Better to live one day wise in meditation than to live a hundred years as a fool. 99
>
> Dhammapada chapter 8, verse 111

Meditation can be done anywhere, but different schools of Buddhism sometimes favour different locations. For example, in Theravada Buddhism, some monks often choose to meditate in a forest. Many Buddhists will visit a temple or monastery on holy days to meditate in front of a statue of the Buddha.

Buddhist monks meditating in front of statue of the Buddha in Laos.

Key vocabulary

jhana A state of absorption – a stage on the path to nirvana through meditation

lotus A flower and key symbol in Buddhism; also used to describe a position used in meditation

Activity

Write a guide to meditation for a Buddhist wanting to find out more about it.

Check your understanding

1. What is meditation?
2. Why might some people say that meditation is not worship?
3. Describe how a Buddhist might practise meditation.
4. Describe how the lotus symbol helps explain the importance of meditation to Buddhists.
5. Describe the jhanas and why some people might struggle to explain them.

Buddhist art

How do Buddhists express their beliefs through art, such as statues, sculptures and mandalas?

Early Buddhists carved scenes from the life of the Buddha into stone and on to cave walls. They believed that it would be disrespectful to show the Buddha as a human, so he is often represented by an empty seat in early Buddhist art. His teachings are often symbolised by a wheel, footprints containing lotus flowers or a royal umbrella or parasol.

Greek stone carvers working in India in the second century CE were the first people to portray the Buddha in human form. Their statues were made to decorate temples and monasteries, but they were also created to teach people who couldn't read Buddhist scriptures about the life and teachings of the Buddha.

The Giant Buddha statue in China is 71 metres tall. It is carved into a mountainside and shows him with long earlobes.

Representations of the Buddha

Statues show the Buddha in different poses each having an important symbolic meaning. Some show the Buddha as starving, which reminds Buddhists that Siddhartha did not find enlightenment through asceticism.

Many statues show him with extremely long earlobes. This may be a reference to Siddhartha's life of luxury as a prince. Wealthy people wore jewellery such as heavy earrings filled with precious stones. These stretched the earlobes, so in early Indian society long earlobes suggested royalty and riches. Statues of the Buddha with elongated earlobes symbolise the Buddhist teaching of the Middle Way and the rejection of luxury. They can also symbolise his compassion and ability to listen.

One of the most famous depictions of the Buddha shows him lying down, or reclining. This reminds Buddhists of the Buddha's death and entry into parinirvana.

Although the Buddha taught people to reject wealth, rich kings and rulers of Buddhist countries have often used expensive materials when creating Buddhist art. One of the most famous examples of this is the Golden Buddha statue in Bangkok, Thailand. The statue is about 700 years old and is made of solid gold. It shows that Buddhists wanted to portray Buddha as an important person, even if such expense conflicts with the teaching of the Middle Way.

The Golden Buddha in Bangkok is worth an estimated £200 million.

There are many other images and symbols of the Buddha. Some show him sitting with his right hand up, the palm facing outwards. This signifies a shield and shows that the Buddha offers protection from suffering. Other statues depict him walking, which signifies the journeys he took to find enlightenment and then to preach the dharma.

Mandalas

Tibetan Buddhism is the school of Buddhism most associated with **mandalas**. Each part of a mandala has a symbolic meaning. In the centre there is usually either a figure (such as the Buddha or Bodhisavattas) or a shape representing a key part of Buddhism (such as compassion, dukkha or wisdom). Around this are four doors through which you can reach the centre. The colours also symbolise important Buddhist ideas. Blue represents the truth of the dharma, white stands for purity and red signifies compassion.

The image of the bhavacakra can be found on the walls of most monasteries and and temples in Tibet.

The most famous Tibetan mandala is the **bhavacakra**, or wheel of life. The being holding the wheel is thought to be Yama, the King of the Dead. The main divisions on the wheel represent the realms into which people can be reborn, including as an animal or a ghost. In the centre are three animals chasing each other in a circle. These represent the Three Poisons of greed, hatred and delusion. In the top right, the Buddha stands outside the wheel, showing that he has achieved nirvana and escaped the cycle of samsara.

> ### Activity
> Draw three different representations of the Buddha and label them to explain what each one means.

> ### Key vocabulary
>
> **bhavacakra** a particular Tibetan Buddhist mandala depicting the cycle of samsara
>
> **mandala** A circular pattern that has symbolic meanings and is used to help people meditate

Making a mandala

Tibetan monks are also famous for constructing beautiful and intricate mandalas using coloured sand. It can take days, weeks or even months to complete, and the monks use special tools to ensure that each grain of sand falls into exactly the right place. These mandalas are displayed during Buddhist festivals. After the festival, the sand is often brushed and mixed together before being collected and poured into a nearby river or stream. This act is also symbolic, demonstrating the Buddhist belief that everything is impermanent.

Check your understanding

1. How did early Buddhist art depict the Buddha?
2. Explain two symbolic ways that the Buddha is represented.
3. What is the bhavacakra?
4. Explain the meaning of the bhavacakra.
5. Explain why Tibetan monks destroy mandalas after they have made them.

Buddhist festivals

Festivals are held to mark important events in the life of the Buddha. Who takes part in these festivals and what happens?

Wesak

Wesak is the most important festival for many Buddhists. In Western countries it is often called 'Buddha Day'. The festival is a time to remember the Buddha's birth, his enlightenment (nirvana) and his death (parinirvana). There is no fixed date for Wesak and it is celebrated at different times in different countries. In most Asian countries, it happens on the first full moon in May. This is because Theravada Buddhists believe that all three events in the Buddha's life took place under a full moon.

Water being poured over a statue of the Buddha during the festival of Wesak.

In countries where Buddhism is the main religion, Wesak is usually a public holiday. Early in the morning, Buddhists visit their nearest temple or monastery, where monks give talks and lead the chanting of mantras, including the Three Jewels. The laity bring gifts of flowers, rice, candles and incense, which are placed by statues or shrines of the Buddha. Some Buddhists also pour water over a statue of the Buddha. This symbolises the washing away of one's past misdeeds and the dousing of the Three Poisons (greed, hatred and delusion).

During Wesak, some Buddhists remind themselves of the importance of the Five Precepts, and others will adopt some extra precepts on the day, such as not eating after midday and not wearing perfume or jewellery. Many Buddhists will mark the occasion by donating to charity or giving free food and drink to those in need.

Vassa

In Theravada Buddhism, the period of **Vassa** lasts for the three months of the Asian rainy season. Monks stay in their monasteries and avoid any travel. It is known as the 'rains retreat' because monks retreat into their monasteries. This tradition dates back to the time of the Buddha and the first Sangha, who stayed in one place as it was too difficult to travel on foot to spread their teachings during this time. During Vassa, monks will practise even more intensive meditation than usual. The laity might choose to give up things like meat and alcohol. This has led some in the West to refer to Vassa as 'Buddhist Lent', although many Christians and Buddhists reject this comparison.

Kathina

Within one month of Vassa ending, the festival of **Kathina** takes place. This is when Buddhists show gratitude to the monks for the end of the rainy season. The origins of Kathina are linked to a legend from the life of the Buddha. According to the legend, a group of 30 monks were travelling to spend the 'rains retreat' with the Buddha. However, the rainy season began before they had finished their journey, so the monks had to stay where they were for three months. After this, they went to see the Buddha. To reward them, the Buddha gave them some cloth and told the travelling monks to turn it into a robe. The Buddha said that they should then decide which of them deserved it. By doing this, the Buddha enforced the idea that monks are not allowed possessions and even their robes must be donated. The story also encourages monks to be self-sufficient by making their own clothes and to show generosity by giving clothes to each other.

During the festival of Kathina, monks are often given gifts of money and cloth.

Gifts to the monks

In some Theravada countries, the laity commemorate this story by taking cloth to monks during Kathina. Usually, one or two monks will accept the cloth on behalf of the rest. The Sangha then spend the day cutting the cloth and fashioning it into robes before deciding which monk will receive the gift. As well as cloth, food, basic sanitary supplies and money are sometimes given to the Sangha. These gifts sustain the monks over the coming year. They are freely given to the monks as a way of saying thank you for the work they do to support the community.

Key vocabulary

Kathina A festival of gratitude to the Sangha

Vassa The period of the rainy season, when monks stay in their monasteries

Wesak A festival to commemorate the Buddha's birth, enlightenment and death; also known as Buddha Day

Check your understanding

1 What three events in the Buddha's life are celebrated at Wesak?

2 When is Wesak celebrated?

3 Explain why some Buddhists mark Wesak by pouring water over a statue of the Buddha.

4 What story from the life of the Buddha is remembered at Kathina?

5 How do the laity show gratitude to the Sangha at Kathina?

Unit 2: Buddhism in the modern world
Places of pilgrimage

What are the main sites of Buddhist pilgrimage and why do Buddhists visit these places?

Just before the Buddha died, he told his followers to remember him by going on pilgrimage to four holy places. These are the sites of his birth, his enlightenment, his first teaching and his death. At all these sites, temples and shrines containing relics of the Buddha have been built. By visiting these places, Buddhists can reflect on the events of the Buddha's life and may feel a stronger connection to him. However, there is no obligation for Buddhists to go on pilgrimage, and many Buddhists never visit pilgrimage sites.

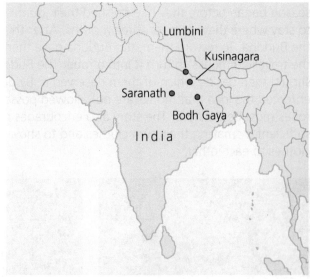

This map shows the locations of the four main sites of Buddhist pilgrimage.

Lumbini

The Buddha's birthplace, Lumbini, is in the foothills of the Himalayas in Nepal. Emperor Ashoka visited Lumbini in the third century BCE. He ordered for the site to be marked with a stone pillar on which was carved 'Here the Buddha was born'. Lumbini was deserted for a long time, but in 1896 a German explorer rediscovered Ashoka's pillar. Since then, the area has remained a place of interest for archaeologists, who try to learn more about the history of Buddhism by studying the remains of buildings and other ancient objects. In recent years, both Theravada and Tibetan monasteries have been established in Lumbini.

> 66 Millions of people get immense inspiration. Buddha's spirit always there. But real Buddha's holy places is in one's self. That's important. So real Buddha's sacred place must build within ourselves. We must build within our heart. 99
> The Dalai Lama on the significance of pilgrimage for Buddhists

A stone marking the site of the Buddha's birth in Lumbini, Nepal.

Bodh Gaya

The most important place in the world for Buddhists is Bodh Gaya, where the Buddha achieved enlightenment. Every year, hundreds of thousands of people visit from all over the world. The main attraction is the Mahabodhi Temple, which is believed to have been built by Emperor Ashoka. At the back of the temple, there is a Bodhi tree. According to legend, the tree is a descendant of the Bodhi tree under which the Buddha found enlightenment. It can be crowded near the tree, but pilgrims often meditate around it, believing that this will help them in their own search for enlightenment. There is also a statue in Bodh Gaya called the Great Buddha. It is 25 metres high and was completed in 1989 after seven years of building by over 12,000 bricklayers.

The Mahabodhi Temple in Bodh Gaya.

Sarnath

On the site of the deer park at Sarnath where the Buddha gave his first sermon stands the Dhamekh Stupa. Pilgrims walk around the Dhamekh Stupa three times, one for each of the Three Jewels. The circle also symbolises the cycle of samsara. Sarnath was a vibrant Buddhist area until it was destroyed in the twelfth century CE by Muslim conquerors. The area was rediscovered in 1937 and is now a thriving Buddhist community again, with many monasteries that pilgrims visit.

The Dhamekh Stupa in Sarnath.

Kusinara

At the site of the Buddha's parinirvana is the Mahaparinirvana Temple and Stupa, which are said to be built on the exact spot that the Buddha died. The ruins of several monasteries can also be found in this area. Buddhist pilgrims also visit the nearby Ramabhar Stupa, where the Buddha was cremated.

Other sites of pilgrimage

The four sites specifically mentioned by the Buddha are usually considered to be the most important, but there are several other sites of Buddhist pilgrimage across Asia. Many people believe that these sites contain relics of the Buddha, including his hair and teeth. These objects prove to Buddhists that the Buddha really existed, and they are a way of connecting with his life and teachings. At some sites there are also ancient monasteries.

Activity

Imagine you have been on a Buddhist pilgrimage to a destination of your choice. Write a diary account of your experience.

Check your understanding

1 What four sites did the Buddha tell his followers they should visit after his death?

2 Which of the four sites is the most important? Explain why this is.

3 Why might Buddhist pilgrims walk around the Dhamekh Stupa three times?

4 What are relics and why are they kept?

5 'All Buddhists should go on pilgrimage.' Discuss this statement.

Unit 2: Buddhism in the modern world
Inspirational leaders

How have inspiring Buddhist leaders helped spread the religion around the world?

Maha Ghosananda

Maha Ghosananda was born into a family of farmers in Cambodia in 1929 and became a novice Theravada monk at the age of 14. He continued his education and training at universities in Cambodia, where he studied under some of the most respected Buddhist masters of his time. Ghosananda travelled and studied in both India and Thailand. While he was living as a monk in Thailand, tragedy unfolded in his homeland.

In 1975, Cambodia was taken over by a group called the Khmer Rouge, led by the dictator Pol Pot. The Khmer Rouge evacuated the cities and sent the people on forced marches to work on special projects in the countryside. In Cambodia, 1975 became year 0, and the Khmer Rouge attempted to rebuild the country's economy based on basic farming. They discarded Western medicine and tried to rid the country of Buddhism by destroying temples, monasteries and libraries. Doctors, teachers, monks, those who spoke a foreign language and anyone who wore glasses were executed.

Ghosananda refused to stand by and do nothing while such terrible things were happening in his country. He left his community in Thailand and worked in refugee camps along the Thailand–Cambodia border. The people he encountered had fled the Khmer Rouge through hazardous jungle. They were so starved of food that Ghosananda described them as walking skeletons. In the refugee camps he built basic Buddhist temples and organised classes where people discussed the Buddha's teachings on forgiveness and compassion.

By the time the Khmer Rouge regime collapsed in 1979, nearly every Buddhist monastery and temple in Cambodia had been destroyed. The Sangha had nearly been wiped out. Prior to 1975, there had been approximately 70,000 monks; in 1979, there were fewer than 3000. Those who had not been murdered were either living secretly among the laity or had fled to other countries. Nearly all of Maha Ghosananda's family and friends were dead.

When Ghosananda returned to Cambodia, he re-established the Sangha. He made contact with monks who had gone into hiding or fled overseas and organised the rebuilding of temples. He became particularly famous for leading an annual 125-mile 'peace walk'. He devoted the rest of his

Cambodia is in Southeast Asia and borders Thailand, Vietnam and Laos.

> **Fact**
>
> Under Pol Pot's regime, it is estimated that at least two million Cambodians, out of a total population of eight million, died from torture, executions, overwork, starvation and disease.

The site in Cambodia known as 'The Killing Fields' where over 8900 people were murdered.

life to encouraging people of different religions to talk to one another and try to understand and respect one another's beliefs. He also campaigned for non-violent solutions to conflict. He was nominated four times for the Nobel Peace Prize. Maha Ghosananda died in 2007.

Maha Ghosananda is sometimes referred to as the 'Gandhi of Cambodia'.

66 Cambodia has suffered deeply.
From deep suffering comes deep compassion.
From deep compassion comes a peaceful heart.
From a peaceful heart comes a peaceful person.
From a peaceful person comes a peaceful family and community.
From peaceful communities comes a peaceful nation.
From peaceful nations come a peaceful world. 99

A poem by Maha Ghosananda in his book *Step by Step* (Parallax Press, 1992)

Thich Nhat Hanh

Thich Nhat Hanh was born in Vietnam in 1926 and became a Buddhist monk at the age of 16. During the Vietnam War, fought between North and South Vietnam, Nhat Hanh called for peace. He also founded an order of monks who made it their mission to help victims of the war. Surrounded by violence, this was often dangerous work.

During the Vietnam War, the USA sent soldiers to support South Vietnam. In 1966, Nhat Hanh travelled to the USA to give speeches against the war, calling for a non-violent solution to the conflict. As a result, Vietnamese leaders banned him from returning to Vietnam. The following year, Nhat Hanh was nominated for the Nobel Peace Prize by Martin Luther King, who greatly admired his intellect and calls for peace.

Today, Nhat Hanh campaigns for peace and social justice from a Buddhist centre he set up in southern France called Plum Village. Many monks, nuns and laity live there and they welcome thousands of visitors a year. The community also interacts with Buddhists around the world via social media. Nhat Hanh was finally allowed to visit his homeland again in 2005.

Thich Nhat Hanh remains a popular teacher of meditation and is the author of over 100 books.

Check your understanding

1. Where is Cambodia?
2. What happened in Cambodia between 1975 and 1979?
3. Explain how Maha Ghosananda helped to re-establish Buddhism in Cambodia.
4. Explain what Maha Ghosananda meant in the quote on this page.
5. Why was Thich Nhat Hanh nominated for the Nobel Peace Prize?

Unit 2: Buddhism in the modern world
Buddhism in the UK

How did Buddhism become established in the UK and how do British Buddhists practise their religion?

History

Today Buddhism is a growing religion in Britain, but for most of the religion's history, it has had no British followers. British people first began taking an interest in Buddhism in the late 1800s, when government workers were sent to work overseas in Buddhist countries. Some of these workers translated Buddhist texts such as the Pali Canon into English. In 1924, a British lawyer set up an organisation called the Buddhist Society in London. Today, the society runs courses and hosts lectures on many different forms of Buddhism. It also has a library containing important Buddhist texts.

After the Chinese invasion of Tibet in 1950, many Tibetan Buddhists came to Britain. The religion's popularity in Britain also grew throughout the 1960s, as people began to travel abroad more often. Many Buddhists living in Britain today have converted to Buddhism from another religion or belief system.

> **❝** I can give my teachings in brief. I can teach in detail. It is those who understand that are hard to find. **❞**
>
> The Buddha

Chithurst

One of the largest Buddhist centres in the UK is in Chithurst, Sussex. The centre's Buddhist name is Cittaviveka, which means 'withdrawn mind'. It is one of five Theravada monasteries in the UK. Cittaviveka was founded in 1979 by a Thai monk. The monastery places an emphasis on following the Five Precepts and other monastic rules while living in a community.

The monastery is part of what is known as the **Thai Forest Tradition**. As such, it has large grounds, mostly made up of woodland containing huts where monks and nuns can retreat and meditate in complete silence and solitude. There are also two houses, one for men and one for women. Men and women tend to stay separate from each other as part of the monastic rules. These houses are used for eating, teaching and accommodating guests who visit the monastery. The monks and nuns live under strict rules. For example, they are forbidden from accepting or even handling money. Like monks in Thailand and Cambodia, a few members of the community go to the local towns and villages to gather donations of food. The community relies heavily on local Buddhists and friends of the monastery for their food and other supplies.

A Sri Lankan Buddhist at Chithurst monastery.

Samye Ling

Samye Ling monastery in southeast Scotland was the first Tibetan Buddhist centre in the West. It was founded in the late 1960s by Tibetan monks who had fled the Chinese invasion of their homeland. Today, it is home to 60 Buddhists.

Those wishing to become monks train themselves in meditation at the monastery for a minimum of 10 years. They learn Tibetan dharma, language and medicine. The monastery is also popular with tourists, who can have guided tours and take part in meditation classes and courses, which can last for a day or over a week. Samye Ling has become well known for creating and restoring **thangkas**. These are Tibetan Buddhist paintings, on cotton or silk, of the Buddha, a Bodhisattva or a mandala.

A statue of the face of the Buddha in the roots of a tree. Many Buddhists feel closest to the dharma in nature.

Rokpa

Buddhists at Samye Ling try to help the wider community. In 1980, the head monk started the Rokpa charity. *Rokpa* is a Tibetan word meaning to help or serve. The charity helps the poorest people in Nepal, especially children. After the 2015 earthquake in Nepal, Rokpa gave emergency supplies and shelter to victims of the disaster.

Buddhism in the UK is diverse, both in terms of how it is followed and where it is located. The rise of the internet and social media means that anyone who is curious can find out about Buddhism and seek guidance on the dharma and meditation. Buddhism has grown into a variety of traditions as it has spread across the world. It is a living faith with a strong message of compassion, personal reflection and understanding. People are still learning and trying to understand the original teachings of the Buddha, 2500 years after his death.

The main temple building at Samye Ling.

Key vocabulary

Thai Forest Tradition A form of Theravada Buddhism that encourages monks and nuns to retreat into the forest to practise meditation in complete solitude

thangkas A Tibetan Buddhist painting on to cotton or silk

Check your understanding

1. How did interest in Buddhism begin in Britain?
2. What is the Buddhist Society and what does it do?
3. Describe the workings of the Buddhist monastery at Chithurst.
4. How did Tibetan Buddhism come to Scotland?
5. Explain the practical work of the Samye Ling community in putting Buddhist beliefs into practice.

Unit 2: Buddhism in the modern world
Knowledge organiser

Key vocabulary

bardo A state of being that exists between death and rebirth

bhavacakra A particular Tibetan Buddhist mandala depicting the cycle of samsara

Bodhisattva A person who has found enlightenment but is reborn to help others

Dalai Lama The leader of Tibetan Buddhism, believed to be an incarnation of the Bodhisattva Avalokitesvara

jhana A state of absorption – a stage on the path to nirvana through meditation

Kathina A festival of gratitude to the Sangha

lama A senior monk or teacher in Tibetan Buddhism

lotus A flower and key symbol in Buddhism; also used to describe a position used in meditation

Mahayana A school of Buddhism that believes in Bodhisattvas and that the term 'Sangha' applies to all Buddhists

mandala A circular pattern that has symbolic meanings and is used to help people meditate

mantra A sacred phrase that is chanted during meditation

Thai Forest Tradition A form of Theravada Buddhism that encourages monks and nuns to retreat into the forest to practise meditation in complete solitude

thangkas A Tibetan Buddhist painting on cotton or silk

Theravada A school of Buddhism that views the Sangha as very important

Vassa The period of the rainy season, when monks stay in their monasteries

Wesak A festival to commemorate the Buddha's birth, enlightenment and death; also known as Buddha Day

Golden statue of Guanyin, a female bodhisattva who embodies the compassion of all Buddhas, at Lushan Temple, China.

Key facts

- Two of the main schools of Buddhism are Theravada and Mahayana. They share many similarities, but Theravada Buddhists place greater emphasis on the Sangha.

- The third main school of Buddhism is Tibetan Buddhism. Tibetan Buddhists have slightly different beliefs, including the belief that between death and rebirth people spend time in a state called bardo.

- The leader of Tibetan Buddhism is the Dalai Lama, who was forced into exile after China invaded Tibet in the 1950s.

- Meditation is a key practice of Buddhists. This involves being still and focusing the mind.

- Buddhists honour the Buddha in art such as huge statues and sculptures and symbolic images such as mandalas.

- The key Buddhist festivals are Wesak (marking the Buddha's birth, enlightenment and death), Vassa (when monks remain in their monasteries during the rainy season) and Kathina (when people celebrate the end of the rainy season by bringing gifts to the monks).

- There are four main sites of Buddhist pilgrimage: Lumbini, Bodh Gaya, Sarnath and Kusinara. These are where Siddhartha was born, enlightened, and as the Buddha taught his first sermon and entered parinirvana.

- The spread of Buddhism in the twentieth century was helped by several inspiring leaders including Maha Ghosananda and Thich Nhat Hanh.

- There are more than 200,000 Buddhists in the UK today. Significant places include the Chithurst and Samye Ling monasteries.

The Golden Wheel of Dharma and Deer sculpture, The Jokhang Temple (most sacred temple in Tibet).

The Dalai Lama is the spiritual leader of the Tibetan people.

Key people

Dalai Lama The spiritual leader of Tibetan Buddhism

Maha Ghosananda A senior monk in Cambodia who helped rebuild the country after war

Thich Nhat Hanh A famous Vietnamese monk who now lives in France

Index

Acknowledgements

Every effort has been made to trace copyright holders and to obtain their permission for the use of copyright material.

The publishers will gladly receive any information enabling them to rectify any error or omission at the first opportunity.

The publishers would like to thank the following for permission to reproduce copyright material:

(t = top, b = bottom, c = centre, l = left, r = right)

Text

The Office of His Holiness the Dalai Lama for a quotation from His Holiness the Dalai Lama, on the significance of pilgrimage for Buddhists, http://www.dalailama.com/. Reproduced with kind permission; Parallax Press for 'A poem by Maha Ghosananda', reprinted from Step by Step: Meditations on Wisdom and Compassion (1992) by Maha Ghosananda with permission of Parallax Press, Berkeley, California, www.parallax.org.

Photographs

Cover and title page Chonlatip Hirunsatitporn/Shutterstock, pp6–7 happydancing/Shutterstock, p8 Nila Newsom/Shutterstock, p10 t Godong/Universal Images Group via Getty Images, p10 b Kittiwongsakul/AFP/Getty Images, p11 British Library/Robana/REX/Shutterstock, p12 t Godong/Alamy Stock Photo, p12 b Granger Historical Picture Archive/Alamy Stock Photo, p13 REX/Shutterstock, p14 Ernst Christen/Shutterstock, p15 Ivy Close Images/Alamy Stock Photo, p16 Yaacov Shein/Alamy Stock Photo, p17 t Pascal Deloche/Getty Images, p17 b TongFotoman/Shutterstock, p18 wikipedia.org, p19 t Albachiaraa/Shutterstock, p19 b weniliou/Shutterstock, p20 James Barr/Alamy Stock Photo, p20 b John Brown/Alamy Stock Photo, p21 Man of the Mountain/Shutterstock, p22 commons.widimedia.org, p23 Chirawan Thaiprasansap/Shutterstock, p25 Hemis/Alamy Stockk Photo, pp26–27 Man of the Mountain/Shutterstock, p28 canan kaya/Shutterstock, p29 defpicture/Shutterstock, p31 t robertharding/Alamy, p31 b Nadezda Murmakova/Shutterstock, p32 Vasin Lee/Shutterstock, p33 t Steve Heap/Shutterstock, p33 b John Brown/Alamy Stock Photo, p34 t imageBroker/Alamy Stock Photo, p34 b Paul Brown/Alamy Stock Photo, p35 t Danita Delimont/Getty Images, p35 b Oleg Konin/REX/Shutterstock, p36 Tim Whitby/Alamy Stock Photo, p37 l Lionela Rob/Alamy Stock Photo, p37 r Stringer/aFP/Getty Images, p38 t Dinodia Photos/alamy Stock Photo, p38 b David Evison/Shutterstock, p39 Saiko3p/Shutterstock, p40 Keith Brooks/Shutterstock, p41 t Dan White/Alamy Stock Photo, p41 b Godong/Alamy Stock Photo, p42 james cheadle/Alamy stock Photo, p43 t Blend Images/Alamy Stock Photo, p43 b Brendan Howard/Shutterstock, p44 Paul Rushton/Alamy Stock Photo, p45 t Alexander Verevkin, p45 b Nadezda Murmakova/Shutterstock.